T0078441

REVELATION OF A MAN

RALPH JOHNSON

WESTBOW
PRESS®
A DIVISION OF THOMAS NELSON
& ZONDERVAN

This book is a work of non-fiction. Unless otherwise noted, the author and the publisher make no explicit guarantees as to the accuracy of the information contained in this book and in some cases, names of people and places have been altered to protect their privacy.

WestBow Press books may be ordered through booksellers or by contacting:

WestBow Press
A Division of Thomas Nelson & Zondervan
1663 Liberty Drive
Bloomington, IN 47403
www.westbowpress.com
844-714-3454

ISBN: 978-1-6642-5854-9 (sc)
ISBN: 978-1-6642-5853-2 (hc)
ISBN: 978-1-6642-5852-5 (e)

Library of Congress Control Number: 2022903388

Print information available on the last page.

WestBow Press rev. date: 07/22/2022

Contents

Warning, Warning

Reading this material can change your morning
And add joy to your day,
Even give you kind words to say—
Can transform your mind set in a storm.
Also, can strengthen you to continue to press on,
And will lead you to disciple others to make
the community spiritually strong.
Please expect resistance from yourself.
But I can promise you will overcome and maintain good health,
And I might add, resistance will be in outside forces as well.
Yes, some people will give you hell.
The battle will start inside your heart.
Once you switch kingdoms, this is nothing new.
The kingdom of light is always true.
New biblical scriptures will give you more eternal insight.
The scriptures will forever give you power and light
As you meditate on them day and night,
And it can change and rebuild your character as you fight.
The number-one thing to do
Will be learning to pray for a breakthrough.
That fire that is in your soul
Comes from the scriptures of old.
As you follow the scriptures' path,
Some days, you will cry, be discouraged, and maybe even laugh.
This race will not be easy.
But be encouraged you don't have to please me.
The kingdom of darkness makes temptation come to you.
And believe it or not, everyone has to go through.
Now that you have read this material through,
This decision belongs to you.
The last thing l will say to you
Jesus or Satan—only one will be master over you.

A Husband's Prayer for Intimacy

Let my words be few as I speak
And take my time to be prayerful as I seek.
Thank you, God, for my marriage,
For you alone created marriage and my wife.
I pray you teach me about this marriage covenant with heavenly insight
Because my heart needs help to manifest your love to my wife.
Teach me how to appreciate my bride,
To love her the way God desires on the inside.
This beautiful, amazing, and wonderful gift—
Who am I to deserve this,
For God to bestow such an excellent creature suitable for me?
Help me, oh Lord, to see and bring out her inner beauty.
That's the Godly image you have created us in.
Teach me on that same level from before Adam sinned
with Eve and submitted to the devil—
How Adam's wisdom and knowledge came straight from God
So when Eve was bestowed to Adam for marriage,
The spirit of the Lord in Adam taught him what to do.
I need your wisdom each day to lead my wife in the kingdom's way.
Your loving mercy and grace can help me encourage my bride today.
Allow me to fast and pray to seek you, oh Lord, to know what to say.
In my marriage, I pray, trying to reflect Jesus's love every day.

The Father of a Special Child

When you are the father of a sick child,
What goes through your mind? Can I go the extra mile?
Why did this happen to me? Can this be fixed?
And what are the possibilities for my child at six?
Can they outgrow this sickness or disease?
I really need some answers, please.
And what do I know? Hit on the blind side, how do I cope?
My emotions are all over the place; you can tell—just look at my face.
And some church folk say, "Where is your faith?"
And can I say, "My mind and body ache"?
For goodness and mercy, heaven's sake.
I have heard of miracles that Jesus performs by people's faith.
Yes, I seem at a loss, whatever the cost.
Will my child make it to their next birthday?
Can they have a normal life with this situation at hand?
And can we as a family love them with all our
might and give them deep insight?
The challenge is present to me, so what will it be?
Will I leave or cleave and help my child to believe
So when they look at me,
They can get all from me that they need?
Some people seem to understand
My positions as the leader and love as a man.
Thank God, who truly understands because he knows me
and my child and thinks way higher than a man.
And Jesus died for all humanity; he is God's redeeming man,
So I can take the love of Jesus and share it with my child the best that I can.

Children Are a Puzzle

Children are heritage from God. Pslam:127-3
Why is that so hard?
Do you believe that from the start?
Can we do our part?
I would say not without God.
We need to humble ourselves
And work with God.
Whether married or single, we need God's help
To build the character of this person together with all our heart.
Pride must be put to the side
To work with this small puzzle every day,
And God knows what's best for you to provide.
Reading books for wisdom is good to do,
And getting good parenting advice will always do;
That bundle of joy is a gift from God.
What a wonderful opportunity we can experience.
We are a steward of God's inheritance,
So let's not be arrogant.
We have to teach these little ones how to connect with God,
And the highest challenge can be giving them back to God.
To lead by example—isn't that where we should stand?
To have them in relationship with Jesus Christ
Is the best thing that could happen to them.
And some may not believe in this at all
Because in this life, we all need someone we can rely on,
And raising a child in this world will always be hard.
Obstacles and things will challenge their heart,
And Jesus is the anchor and foundation when they fall.
But we must love them through it all
So they can answer when Jesus will call.

Your Kids

What kind of impression did you make on your kids?
Did you spend the time with your kids?
Did you spend a dime on your kids?
Did you cultivate the time you had with your kids?
To invest in their future is always good,
Connecting with their spirits and minds the way you should.
This time will come back with a deposit of
interest, and I hope it will do you good.
This reward you can't afford to miss.
Your kids need this time, so don't you stop.
There is no good reason you should forget.
They really, truly need this.
So don't gamble; you can't replace this.
Money gifts can't find a space in this.
You are the meaningful time in their lives.
Their future is real; it depends on this.
We need know amazing power; just spend time with them one hour.

My Teenage Daughter

Can I please have a tall glass of water?
My daughter has a boyfriend.
It's no time to scream and shout.
My daughter has a boyfriend; sometimes, I think about helping her out.
She thinks he's a dream.
I just hope they order ice cream.
A first-time relationship can be mean.
I mean, what can I say, that girl is green.
Feet are not firmly planted on the ground; her mind is not sound.
Her emotions are very high; I just want to die.
I try to give her some good old-fashioned advice.
She rolls her eyes and looks into the sky.
I am twice as nice,
But then I lose my vice.
Then I pray to God to do what is right.
I even ask my wife for some female advice.
She has great self-esteem,
But in a relationship, this can melt like ice cream.
Why did God give me a daughter?
I guess this was his order.
I will always love my daughter.
My prayer for her is what God has to offer.
My wife says that we should support her;
This is what you do for your daughter.
God's principles are always in order.
This is how I learned to support my daughter.
My daughter has a boyfriend; I don't need a review.
I pray that she will understand God's Word and I can be
an encouragement to her as she goes through.

How Do You Honor Your Wife?

This question has a lot of meaning in life.
Begin to meditate on the wedding vows you spoke into her life.
Dissect each word for new meaning in your married life.
What kind of service do you provide?
Are you on call twenty-four hours a day to be a blessing to your bride?
Do you understand your life is given to your wife for the rest of your life?
You must try to give one hundred percent of your total being to her life,
Honoring and cherishing your wife.
Become a good listener to your wife.
Be strong emotionally with her and get closer
and overcome those petty fights.
Speak good things into her life.
Praise her when she may be trying to get it right.
Do this morning, noon, and night.
Try for more understanding to support her life.
Put her needs before your life.
Try to make the ultimate sacrifice to show appreciation to your wife.
Make her feel special every day of her life.
Be creative in what you do, and say to her as your wife.
Emotionally connect with her, and speak peace in her life.
If you are a spiritual man of God, guide her with Jesus Christ.
Be an example of Jesus Christ each day of her life.
You can be that miracle she needs this night
And bridge the gap that she may have more of the abundant life.
If you have kids or a baby, show a double portion
of love to her with no maybe.
Telling her you love her is fine, but more action
mixed with it gives her peace of mind.
And ask God for new wisdom every day so he can give
you a new revelation to love her in a special way.

Marriage Will Have Conflict

Yes, marriage will have conflict, but be advised this is not a trick.
A couple will see and hear things that bring conflict.
Oh, well, this can be a bombshell
Because some married couples are really not prepared.
Fear and anger can get emotionally involved in their head.
It can turn into World War Three, trust and believe me.
And by the way, I am not trying to give marriage a bad reputation.
This is a reality, but some couples have not comprehended this information.
And maybe at this time, I am describing you.
So what can we do to remedy this conflict flu?
Let's try not to get paranoid about this situation
As I will try to administer this helpful information.
If we can anticipate and make the necessary adjustments with our mate,
Then that conflict flu will not have the same old symptoms in you.
Let me share a truth with you:
Conflict is common in marriage; this isn't new.
But how we resolve conflict can be essential to your spouse and you,
And premarital counseling—I would recommend this for you.
And marriage seminars and workshops are good for couples to continue.
This way, you can strengthen your marriage and repair it too
So when conflict arises, you and your spouse will know what to do.

People Who Are Married

I talk to some men and women,
And they both sound the same:
Something in their marriage went wrong,
And their heart isn't quite the same.
They all seem to say,
"I will never, ever get married again."
Is marriage a bad institution?
Marriage can't be that bad.
I mean, look at all the blessings two people have
If you have God's love for marriage plus the bad.
All things have hope and promise.
God's Word has made me glad.
God's love is the motivating factor,
And this key ingredient we need to have.
We need God's love growing and being cultivated in our hearts.
I know bad things can crop up,
Like anger, bitterness, and unforgiveness.
These things can tear us apart.
That's why we must both give God our hearts—
To open our heart to see
The blueprint God has designed for us.
Marriage is God's family unit as well as the church.
So how are your family fundamentals?
And do you have God's principles?
Because biblical marriage counseling is the best way to go.
God's plan for marriage will help the family unit grow.
And with God's love and commands,
We can face any problem the world can't stand.
Marriage originated from God.
This is where we should start.
Marriage is in the heart of God.
So we can study God's Word on marriage
And apply it from our heart.

My Divorce

Of course people get a divorce.
God has nothing to do with divorce.
Sinful nature from the devil contributes to this source.
I personally don't believe in divorce; before you settle for a
divorce, I recommend biblical counseling, of course.
But I do understand why some people get a divorce.
It's a shame where we try to place all the blame.
Sometimes, it even gives us a bad name.
I can't describe all the side effects it may have on your brain
And your heart and mind, fighting not to go insane,
And outsiders asking, "Who is to blame?"
Thank God for his mercy on our soul.
We need his grace and mercy and love to repair and take control.
And some people look at you like you're dumped,
Especially if you say, "I've been divorced more than once."
But I know this to be true:
You can live life with or without pain; this is up to you.
You are single now.
Please don't let this divorce get the best of you.
I have been divorced twice, so what did I do?
I went through the uncomfortable process just like you.
You have to choose what's best for you.
Stop blaming and feeling sorry for yourself; that won't do.
I pray that this poem will help motivate divorced people to make it through.
I looked to God for help, and he coached me to pursue
The things that God has for me to do.
God told me the issues of life are in the heart.
There's life before marriage
When you get married,
And life after divorce too.
It was hard for me, and maybe it's hard for you.

But remember, God got me through more than
one divorce; he got me through two.
So what have I learned, and is there anything to share with you?
God is still performing marriages in the land, and his testimonies
Are true.
And God has a will for your life, so what are you going to do?

The Revelation of a Man

What is revealed in a man?
And where does his purpose stand?
What makes him evolve?
Can we influence man?
And does his environment affect the way he thinks and plans?
What is a man?
And how does our society reveal man?
How much education has he been exposed to in his generation?
And what can we do to help the fallen man?
Does the image of man look dim?
Is he consistently working in sin?
How do you see men in society today?
What does your perspective say?
We have no perfect solution for man this day.
Didn't God create man in his image to stand?
Now, does man have a desire to follow God's commands?
And yes, there are some men who are making a difference in our land.
What are their strengths and weaknesses?
We need to work together to help our community.
How are the young men being trained to grow up today?
And yes, some of our role models have gone their own way.
I simply believe the answer for us won't come from the dust.
Every man needs a solid spiritual foundation.
Where there is a weak nation, there is no solid spiritual foundation.
Fear not; God truly understands what it takes for a boy to become a man.
That's why he sent Jesus to us—God's ultimate plan.
The true revelation of a man can only be revealed
by God, who truly created man.
So what can we learn about the revelation of a man?
Pray and trust God to give us the heart of grace to better understand.

The Character of a Man

What is in the character of a man?
Does this include others as he expands?
Is he leading followers to the right command?
Do most of his thoughts work with people in his plans?
Many titles of man,
But titles can become idles of a man.
Can he follow as well as he leads?
And how well does he read?
Is there value for family in his heart?
Does he finish all of his projects before he departs?
Are women respected to the highest regard?
Is he a protector of women's and children's rights from the start?
Can he make sound decisions?
Or is he causing much division?
Does he take care of others' needs before his own?
Or is he gossiping to others on the phone?
Does he serve God
Or serve himself? That's not that hard.
Does he encourage and motivate you
Or talk about himself and the job that he can do?
After you have been around him for a month or two,
Can other people see him for the things you do?
Do you hear good things about his past when
his old friends cross your path?
Do you think his character is good for you?
Or do you feel emotionally drained when he is around you?
Is his personality unreal?
Or can you see genuine appeal?
And how do you really emotionally feel?
The character of a man is his true spirit of who he is,
So don't fall head over heels in love with him yet.
Study that character, my pet.

And ask about what they think of it.
Don't be shy, and please don't lie.
Be true and evaluate just what you see
Because the character of man is on the inside,
not the outside of what you see.

How Does a Man Think?

What shall a man think?
And what burdens do you share?
Where's your conversation going, and why do you care?
If you are not thinking about others,
Then what's on your mind?
Because before you help anyone, you need to combine,
And leading others does become rain or shine.
We need men to take the lead and to work with others at their own speed.
Thinking good thoughts can be hard to do
Because so much garbage is out here in life, but this is nothing new,
Making a conscious effort so we can follow or know when to lead.
How you think and what you know sometimes
can tell me how far you will go.
Good thinking can be motivating and encouraging.
Some folks focus on what others say.
And then there are those who think about nothing constructive all day,
Wasting time and brainpower the good Lord gave us; we need to pray
So we can use the mind the good Lord gave us this day.

The Burden of a Man

Oh, man, what is upon you?
And what has separated you from the crew?
What are you thinking or trying to do?
Can you shake this thing off from you?
Because some burdens stick like glue.
Do other men feel this burden coming from you?
How do you express your point of view?
A burden can be fair if someone only truly cares.
Or sometimes, people stop, look at you, and stare,
Expressing what you feel, and try to make it plain.
Sometimes, it seems like you are just lame.
People can nod their head, but that doesn't mean
they understood a word you have said.
Honestly, it can drive me crazy at times.
These unknown burdens steer my heart and mind.
I even try to share them with my wife.
Sometimes, she gets it; other times, not on your life.
Then I am right back to the drawing board again.
At times, family and friends think the same:
"He's nice but just a little insane."
What is wrong with me?
Is this normal for a man,
To carry a deep emotional burden?
Okay, what can this be? Is this hereditary for me?
I can't sleep or eat until I put this burden to sleep.
Some people may think I need professional help.
Let's go higher than man and see God's wisdom and command.
I really, truly need a burden bearer.
Jesus quoted—"My yoke is easy and my burdens are light."
I will try to give this burden to Jesus before I
go to sleep tonight. Mathew 11-28

In the Heart of Man

Oh, man, what's in your heart for a wife?
Can she become a part of your life?
Are you open to work with her day and night
To construct and help renovate her life?
Will her words soothe your soul and make you whole?
Are her words sweet to hear when she says things to keep you clear?
If I close my eyes, and listen to what she has to say,
will the words from her lips uplift my day?
Is her inner beauty God's delight?
Is she dedicated to work on it day and night?
Can she find things to do that would make me say God is true?
If all I can see is her outer beauty, then what else is key?
I pray that her inner beauty will do exactly what God created it to do.
And hopefully, she will be a blessing to God, me, and others too.
Sometimes, what I desire in a woman seems hard to find.
So I pray to God, and he gives me peace of mind.

What's in Your Head?

Can you tell me what's in your head?
And yes, based on what you said,
We need an emergency CAT scan to X-ray your head.
And how are you led—
By thoughts that are running around in your head?
Based on what you said, what are you doing to be fed?
Because your thoughts can be fed by others who are misled.
What's on your mind at this time?
Is there foolishness on your mind?
Are your thoughts going against God at this time?
Are you having thoughts about committing a crime?
If you get caught, will you do the time?
Are you spiritually blind?
Let's squash this illegal mind
And replace it with a life that's best designed
So you can show faith your best state of mind
And others can see you shine.
With that new responsible peace of mind,
Your life will have new meaning and purpose at this time,
And your commitment to keep a positive frame of mind.
Just keep renewing it all the time.
And ask God for endurance; it's a guaranteed life insurance.

A Self-Centered Man

What can I say? He has a plan
To worship himself in an everyday demand,
And making sure that self-satisfaction is a high-level command. 2Tim:3:2-5
Everybody else rides on the outside of your pride.
You really believe it's about you and only you,
But we all know this is not true.
So what do you think we ought to do?
Don't let it get to us; this isn't new.
Thank God we are more mature than that; please tell me this is true.
And please don't tell me you have children in the mix.
I know you see nothing wrong with this.
You can get mad, but I see a very immature dad.
It's not cool he has some people fooled.
He thinks the world revolves around him because
he's the man in popular demand.
There are some things he just doesn't understand.
He is on his throne and giving out orders all day long on his cell phone.
We should pray really hard.
And if you have Jesus's faith,
Let's turn him over to God
Because other than that, he can make your life very miserable.
Then you may start getting some illegal thoughts.
If this is your dad or brother, I hope you have a praying father or mother.
Something from God needs to humble his will.
Continue to pray without ceasing and follow God's plan
Because hopefully, this person may change or turn back into sand.

I Do

What do you do?
I do understand that I am a man.
What type of man, and can you please explain?
Male by birth, born on this earth,
Changing by God so I can do my part.
I do need Jesus to help me live this life
Because I really need to change on the inside day and night.
I try to do my best,
Yes, with all my human strength of my breath.
I am here to work; that's how God made me.
And that's why Jesus saved me.
I do believe Jesus is the Son of God.
I do receive and believe Jesus came to earth.
I do know some days, I truly don't understand my
mission from God to follow his plan
And to follow Jesus Christ by faith.
To love and help others is the command.
What a job I have as a man.
It would be good if more people supported this plan.
But reality is short of demand.
One leopard came back to thank Jesus for healing him, one out of ten.
I do understand that I need to always pray for myself and my fellow man.
Some people really don't appreciate God's salvation plan.
Jesus found me in my sin,
And his mercy and grace taught me from within
To be a disciple and follow Jesus's commands.
Jesus doesn't want me to live in sin,
So I do try following him from within.
But I do sometimes fall short and sin.
And Jesus's love is right there again and again to
forgive me and help me overcome my sin.
So I say, "I do," to the covenant Jesus made for me, and
try to serve God in every way to please him.
No man can say, "I do," without true commitment to be renewed.

Darkness Is in the Land

Is darkness in the heart of a man?
I dedicate this to every victim who died by the hand of human being.
Some spiritual things we don't understand.
And justice isn't in the heart of a wicked man.
We push to live again to start our life over again.
Why did this happen to our loved ones? Who can truly help us understand?
The hurt, the pain we live day to day,
Trying to make sense of this tragic event every day.
Who can comfort us in this way?
Our burden is heavy even when we pray.
Some victims escape to live; thank God for them.
Please understand wicked people do live in the land.
We find out others can share our burden that identifies with our pain.
Things do happen for a reason even if we can't figure it out.
We ask God why these situations take place;
Evil has come and manifested this act in this way.
We can try to pray to see what God will have to say.
And sometimes, bitterness and anger are hard for us to get away.
But the reality is we can't live this way.
We have no clue what to do.
The grief is hard for you to get some relief.
We definitely need God every day.
God is all knowing, wise, and eternal.
God has always been in love with us; that's why he sent Jesus to us.
Jesus's life that he lived on earth is for all people to benefit.
There is a spiritual battle going on in the earth,
And it has been taking place since our birth—
Spiritual darkness trying to dominate the earth.
But Jesus came and broke that curse
So we can live victorious here on earth.

How Good Do I Think I Am?

Well, how good are you?
Am I a good person? Let me ask your friends,
Or maybe I can ask a sibling this information,
Your spouse; either way, there is a simple explanation.
What have we been taught?
How do we process this thought?
And are we as good as we think we are, or is this infatuation?
Who is all that good?
Are we good according to human interpretation?
Now, Jesus was considered good on all expectations,
And did miracles without human explanation.
Jesus went about doing good and healing all who were sick. Act:10-38
I have heard people say I'm a good person.
But what is their definition?
If people are good, does sin make them bad?
Because everyone sins, even the saints; I know this makes some people mad.
Unselfishly helping others—
That would be a Good Samaritan; one day, a
man addressed Jesus as *good rabbi.*
The Bible states don't think more highly of yourself than you ought.
Think of yourself with sober judgment in accordance
with the faith of God. Rom:12-3
If you believe in Jesus's goodness, then God is the Author.
How good do I think I am,
Still learning each day according to God's Word?

Is This My Position?

Or do I need a new commission?
Are there any open positions?
What is my standard opposition?
Being human. So what do I do?
What do I say, and who do I listen to?
Take orders and watch the borders.
Do I judge others, how they live?
Can I make excuses so I can think big?
By what principle do I live?
What is your position in this life?
Do you continue to argue with your wife?
Have you found your position,
Or are you still looking for permission?
What's your passion?
Maybe that's the problem in life.
We don't know where we are in this life.
It's okay if you don't know.
Just take time to try to make sure.
Then let's start again
To see if you can impact life.
This time, you can team up with your wife.
To know where you stand
Can help you as a man,
No matter who you are,
Knowing your position is like a star
And how significant you are.
Get into your position, and start a brand-new edition.

My Expectation of You

What are my expectations, and are they true?
Do I have genuine principles to see them through?
Deep down, are my expectations sound,
Or do they have me going around?
Have my expectations of someone come short? Didn't report.
Do I expect what is fair?
And if not met, do I pull out my hair?
Some people really don't even care.
We stress to be blessed.
If we only confess, we overestimate our guest.
Then we look for a return with interest and stick out our chest.
But the reality of this mess is that people will come not to bless.
People love to be blessed,
Not so much to give this in depth.
Please don't build false expectation,
Because people always have a lot of expectations.
And some people have a false reputation
In and outside of these United Nations.
Please check for fruit of their reputation
And examine all of the pertinent information.
Then and only then, you can make a good observation
To try to have good expectations.
Then I will say to you congratulations.

Can You Take Correction?

Maybe not to your perfection.
Are you running for your own election?
Does your pride keep you from correction?
But you love to give other people correction,
And you always give a thorough inspection
Before you give out your correction.
Sometimes, you're very critical of my explanation.
Then we end up in a bitter confrontation.
I will admit sometimes it's helpful information,
But not when I am trying to have a normal conversation.
I think it all boils down to your relationship.
How much will a little patience play into this?
And don't get me wrong; correction helps one become wise and strong,
But not all day long.
Where's the balance in the quarrel?
You weren't born to correct everything I do.
This I know from God to be true.
But some of the same mistakes I make, you make too,
And when I bring them to your attention, you say this is not true.
Whether you believe it or not,
You should know this to be true,
For the same measure you give out will come back to you.
It appears to me that some people who like to give
correction have a very bad reception.
Maybe if they received it more, they would be less likely to be critical.
I say if you can take correction, then you are able to give some.

Perfection

Is this your deception?
Do you think you can work to perfection?
Are you working in this direction?
Can you see your reflection?
Is there human perfection?
Do you believe in God's resurrection?
Isn't God Lord over perfection?
Is God included in your perfection?
God's principles work with true perfection.
God's Word can help you get out of any deception.
His Word is even used for your correction.
It will lift you out of your depression.
Can God's Word fail you? That is totally out of the question.
God's Word is who he is, with all love and expression.
Trust me when I say this: God's Word is truly a blessing.
His Word will help you live up to his expectation
Because you are his number-one creation.

Do You Conform, or Do You Transform?

Do you peel the potatoes or eat the skin?
Do you give people bad advice, cause them to sin?
Or do you stand steadfast in the face of adversity from within?
Will you speak up when it is time to begin?
Or will you cave in and conform to peer pressure once again?
Thinking of moving forward, my friend?
Can you see the optimistic situation from within?
Are people intimidating you when the challenge begins?
If this describes you, let's take a look from within.
You can be a flickering candle that refuses to go out;
The strength of your will can never be blown.
Black slaves built America, but some transformed their way to break free.
Slaves transformed into American culture that rejected
them by law and said they would be slaves for life.
But some slaves knew God and would show some Americans
what God created men and women to be.
American history tried to conform African people
to what they wanted them to be.
From the time you are born is new hope that you will
transform and be all that God wants you to be.
Sometimes, people will conform and not transform
family friends or their society.
Jesus was a carpenter who transformed into the
Messiah and became the Savior of the world.
You have a choice each day to transform or conform
your day to what you want it to be.
I am grateful to God, family friends, and people
in history who transform life for me.
Now, it's our turn to transform or conform—what's it gonna be?

Computer World

Has the computer world rocked our world?
Is it a gem or a pearl?
Has it crept up and robbed every boy and girl?
Has it taken over our world?
Can I do anything without signing off or on?
When was the computer world really born?
The computer baby isn't all bad.
It has its good times.
Then sometimes, it's quite sad.
Do we rely on the computer too much?
Does man have a hunch?
Where does the computer society go to lunch?
Has modern technology given us the crunch?
Can I do anything without this machine,
My computer, or do I have a dream?
It wasn't always this way.
We had a social life; computers had no say.
Is the computer a new friend in this modern-day life?
You say, "No way, that's crazy," but let me ask your wife.
Have computers come to save the day?
Or is it Jesus's job that made away?
Don't get me wrong; the computers are great in some things they do,
As long as they don't replace God, me, or you.

When There Is No One to Talk To

Why can't I find anyone to talk with?
Because you are out of options and people don't understand.
Now, God is different; his thoughts aren't like man's.
And the words he will give you will help you plan.
Now, pay attention to the truth that will unfold out of God's hand.
If there is anyone who understands, God can.
God sent Jesus to us from heaven to earth,
And the stories about Jesus are amazing, starting with his birth.
God's Word can keep you
Because God loves you better than you.
And God wants a personal relationship with you that will never end.
Jesus and God's Word go hand in hand.
But our hard-heartedness and disobedience can reject God's command,
Wanting to control our own world.
Nah, but the devil has deceived, and some people do believe.
We are stewards over what God has created.
So who is governing your life?
Why should we talk to God?
Because man is slowly falling apart.
Sin is destroying people from the heart.
God created man and woman in his image—
what a wonderful work of art—
And gave us a free will to serve him; now that's an awesome God.
Shall we obey God and take Jesus at his word
Or ignore Jesus and go against his commands?
This is the choice we have every day
To listen to God's voice, honor Jesus, and obey.
Then the love will grow, and talking to God will bless your soul.

The Heart

How's your heart beating?
Is it slow or fast?
Do you think you will last?
Does your heart reveal the truth you need?
Right now, where is your heart at this time?
Maybe you are heartbroken; make no mistake, your heart is not open.
Yes, you can be heartsick from all of this.
Are you afraid to be heartfelt because people can make your heart melt?
Isn't it true Jesus can hearten your heart and bring you through?
Are you experiencing heartache because of the emotional
disconnect from your faith or family?
Is your heart rending from people in your family or church members?
Can we have heartstrings ever again?
Heart stopping at this time—maybe it's your last beat or a sign.
The heartbeat is a beautiful sound that God made so we can be profound.
Jesus came to heal the brokenhearted. Luke4:16-19
Have you had a heart-to-heart talk with Jesus yet?
If you haven't, please, I pray, give some time to do so.
It will change your life.
Jesus will give you a heart checkup,
A biblical prescription to keep your heart spiritually healthy
No matter who you are or what sins you may have committed.
Jesus came for the brokenhearted.
And yes, Jesus can heal your heart.

What Is Sin?

An offense against God.
How can you live and not acknowledge God?
God is very much alive.
We act like we are in charge.
Sin won't give us a relationship with God.
It only hardens our heart,
And this drives us further apart.
How can we actually live independent from God?
Sin is hereditary; it's birthed in our heart.
Do we truly understand what sin is?
Having offense against God—is this how we should live?
God never made it this way.
We have decided to make a choice and go our own way.
Do we feel and think this is okay?
Can we truly survive or even thrive?
How can we live outside of what God has made?
Sin is deceptive and very unkind.
It's bold, and it will control and take over your mind.
You may be living well and think everything is fine.
But outside of God, is life actually divine?
I know having a solid job, a spouse, a good place to live—
Or even having these things, a great career and kids—
These things are good to have in life,
But what about experiencing God, the only true giver of life?
What about a relationship with Jesus Christ in this daily life?
Because the wage of sin is death,
There are consequences if we want to live in sin.
Is this how we want our life to end,
Controlled and dominated by sin?
There is nothing good at all about sin.
Sin's job is to steal, kill, and destroy,
And this is nothing to take lightly.
The devil is the author of this sinful spirit of deceit,
And anyone who follows him will get the same defeat.

God has a place for the devil to be.
When the world comes to an end, you will see.
And Jesus will come back again to place the devil under his feet.
Hell is the place where he and his demons will go,
And if people haven't given Jesus their heart before the world ends,
They, too, will enter hell with much grief and disbelief. 2Cor.5-12

Falsely Accused

Have you ever been falsely accused
Of something you would never do?
And did you know the allegation that was against you?
Well, this was my plight.
And it lasted seven months of my life.
I had a long week that week.
But this particular weekend would knock me off of my feet.
It was Sunday evening, to be exact,
When my confusion started with one simple act.
I was asked to leave the premises and not come back.
To my surprise, I followed instructions and never went back.
I tried to figure out this scene.
With no explanation, I didn't understand this act.
I drove home like that.
Started racking my brain, but the stress still remained.
Didn't really know what to do—has this ever happened to you?
Called my brother after a while.
He said, "This isn't good," and I thoroughly understood.
Now, at that time, four weeks had passed.
With unanswered questions, my dilemma continued to last.
Then I prayed to God with supplication to unfold this mysterious situation.
Praise God, my friend called and had an answer for me the next day.
I tried to wrap my mind around what was said,
But I kept getting disarray in my head.
Even though I didn't commit this crime,
Innocent people go to jail all of the time.
Then I had some uninvited guest, law enforcement, at my address.
The investigation seemed to be long,
And the questions they asked continue on.
My brain was anticipating a verdict at this time.
I meditated on scriptures each day,
And God gave me peace of mind.
Praise to my Lord and Savior on that day
When the detective called and said they had dropped the case.

It's the Truth

Okay, you are right.
It is the truth.
But what right do you have to set it loose?
It's not compassion; why are you speaking?
So what's your motive? Why are you trying to play me cheap?
Why the tongue lashing?
Can you justify the awful bashing?
And why are you sharing my personal information?
By what authority and rights do you stand?
And what is our relationship built upon—a rock or sand?
Do you think this is right,
That you do this in full spite?
But what gives you the right to judge my truth?
Justification—you have no right to give me a presentation.
Thanks, but no thanks.
Your spirit is not right,
And I didn't ask for your opinion.
But you have forced my truth upon my ears,
Not respecting my wishes of what I didn't want to hear.
Knowing my truth doesn't make you my judge.
And to slam me with it—what, does that make you right?
You just want to read me
Because your ego is saying, "Feed me."
Your pride has no compassion; that's why your heart gave me a thrashing.
Today me, tomorrow you.
If you don't believe, you will humbly receive.
Some of the best things are words that have been spoken right.
The strength of encouragement—that's right.
Speak into my life what is right,
And God will bless you overnight.

God and Man

What is the master plan?
Is God a man?
No, thank God,
He is not a man. Num:23-19
God made man; this is a wonderful plan,
To preach the gospel in the land
So people don't know God's salvation plan.
What's between God and man?
And what is trying to stop the master plan?
Sin separates God from man,
But Jesus is the glue within the plan.
He also came from a miracle birth
To reconcile man back to God.
Satan tries to block that plan
By planting seeds of deception to every man.
God loves the soul of man.
We were made to follow God's plan.
People, don't get me wrong; women and children also belong.
They are all a part of God's salvation plan.
People, if you don't know what to do,
If you don't have Jesus in your heart, this is what you do:
Repent of sin to God now so Jesus can help you grow in his spirit.
And if you don't repent of sin, it will continue to control you from within.
What's in between God and man?
Either sin or Jesus; it's in your hand.
Yes, a relationship with God Jesus can do for you,
Or a life of sin. What's new?
You have a choice to make; it's up to you.

Jesus

Does that name sound familiar to you?
And yes, I know he was a Jew.
So what's your point of view?
Don't hold back now; what do you think? And don't shrink.
Do you think Jesus was a rebel?
Because some folk called him the devil
And said he was making all kinds of trouble.
And he spoke on another level.
First of all, do you believe he exists?
Because some folk think he is a myth,
Came as a baby, a virgin birth.
The Bible prophesied that the Messiah would come to us on earth,
Healed all who were sick of any disease,
And was a perfect gentleman and served people's needs,
Didn't break one single law. Isaiah:9:6-7
People asked what was Jesus's flaw.
Pharisees said blasphemy, but no, they were wrong,
Doing the will of his father, God, all day long.

What Is Love?

It comes to seek and find
And teach you to have peace of mind.
Love will search until it can't search anymore.
Love will find the best in you even down to the core.
Love has made a deep commitment to help,
And love will transfer its resource to see you prosper.
Love will encourage you to the highest level,
And love will overcome darkness and defeat the devil.
Love will stand the test of time.
Love is patient, good, and kind,
And perfect love is always on time. 1Cor:chapter13
This perfect love brings out the bright sunshine.
It can even help you when you are in a bind.
This love can be used at all times.
It's a choice that we make at the right time.
Is this that love that comes from above?
It brought Jesus from heaven. Is this God's love—
Jesus, the Word of God that became flesh?
Love is Jesus, committed to what God said he would do,
And God the father is always committed to the truth.
That's why love is always trying to bring out the very best in you.

Disciple

There are many disciples in life
But only one group that will follow Jesus Christ.
Which one are you in life?
Are you following another master, not Jesus Christ?
A disciple who leaves no doubt what Jesus is all about,
Consistently praying for lost souls to come to Jesus,
Trying truly to be honest with the Holy Spirit's conviction of sin,
Dealing with conflict and circumstances once again?
And I try to pray every day to understand.
When I have failed and sin before God,
I try to get back up, but sometimes, it seems hard
To draw closer to God and confess my sin.
Being a disciple of Jesus Christ's is not an easy life,
But I try to follow Jesus's life,
This new and improved spiritual life.
Just be prepared for spiritual warfare, to fight.
And try to walk in God's Word in this life,
Trying your very best to be like Jesus Christ.
I pray that the Holy Spirit will refresh your life.

The Glory of God

Who can tell the story of God's great splendor and glory?
Heaven's angels recognize God's majesty.
Everything that was made by God's hands speaks of his sovereignty.
Even our birth on planet Earth tells of the extraordinary wisdom of God.
The smallest insect to the largest mammal he has created.
All of the wonderful sights and the beauty of
nature, we see blueprints of his glory.
If we can just begin to try to comprehend all of
the marvelous things that God has done
And not take for granted, no, not even one
In heaven and under the sun.
The universe and galaxy God has fashioned and designed,
And every living creature was formed and given life from God.
That's why all of nature and creation sings to honor and recognize
the authority of Jesus Christ, our everlasting king,
Defeated the devil here on earth at his best.
Jesus gave us the key to life, and now I'm blessed.
Don't know too much, but I can say I'm blessed,
Trying to follow Jesus's example nevertheless.

Thank You, God

Thank you, God, for being the one.
Thank you, God, for sending Jesus, your Son.
Thank you, God, for Jesus Christ.
Thank you, God, for abundant life.
Thank you, God, for anointing Jesus, your Son.
Thank you, God, for faithfulness toward your creation.
And thank you, God, for forgiveness of sin to all generations.
Thank you, God, for your loving ways.
Thank you, God, for you will never change.
Thank you, God, for your spoken word.
Thank you, God, for the powerful messages I have heard.
Thank you, God, for Jesus teaching your Word.
Thank you, God, for Jesus being that written Word.
Thank you, God, for Jesus being the Lamb of God
who takes away the sins of the world.
He died on the cross for souls that were lost.
Thank you, God, that Jesus rose from the grave.
Thank you, God; now, we all can be saved.

Why Do I Pray?

For people to experience abundant life.
Why do I pray?
That pastors acknowledge God every day.
Why do I pray?
To become more like Jesus each day.
Why do I pray?
To get God involved in our lives this day.
Why do I pray?
Because this is the best way.
Why do I pray?
Because it changes my life as I pray.
Why do I pray?
God always responds when I pray.
Why do I pray?
To talk to God this day.
Why do I pray?
I wouldn't have it any other way—
To help me see Jesus this very day.
Why do I pray?
To show me my true self each day.
Why do I pray?
So Jesus can help me overcome my day.
Why do I pray?
To do my job better this day.
Why do I pray?
For peace of mind this day.
Why do I pray?
To get along with church folk this day.
Why do I pray?
For answers to my questions this day.
Why do I pray?
For my friend in India—Jesus will bless his day.
Why do I pray?
For other countries to receive Jesus, and he will lead the way.

Prayer Will Bring You Through

Prayer for many generations has changed people and destinations.
Prayer changes history quite a bit.
Prayer can take on any hit.
Prayer is always the number-one thing to do
Even if we think we know what to do.
Prayer connects us with God's truth.
Prayer can strengthen and encourage us in any trial or tribulation.
Some people find this quite odd.
Why would we talk to a Supreme God?
Because this is our inheritance from God—
To be a part of God's love and dominion from the start.
Prayer connects us to the heart of God
Because God's words are from his heart.
The Bible is God's love letter to us
To see things from God's perception.
So would you like to start to pray and build a relationship with God today?
You say, "Not right now—maybe another day."
It's okay; that's why we pray. To get people on
the same page is a miracle any day.
Prayer gets God involved in our lives.
Some men, women, children, widows, and orphans desire to pray.
They are all looking to God for love, hope, and new
opportunities to change their lives this day.
My God gives them endurance to pray for a breakthrough.
I must say people by nature normally won't pray.
Situations and circumstances can give people motivation to pray.
God has given his people a burden to pray,
And sometimes, we must labor in prayer.
This takes deep commitment, determination, and
dedication in God to endure some prayers.
We can take a stand and fight in prayer.
Whatever it takes, we love to pray
To see God's will take place in the earth each day.
So I encourage you to pray with God's passion for others
And stand in the gap for people who need prayer.

Why Do I Try?

Can someone tell me the reasons why—
The method of my own demise?
If I don't try, then I can never realize
What things I can accomplish from the inside.
Sometimes, it's my stubborn pride that keeps me a prisoner on the inside.
The things that God has for me are alive,
So I try to reach these things before I die.
Some folks just give up and deny
And think, *Why should we try?*
But God's hope gives me lots of good reasons why
To make it work again.
This time, I will try
So I can help a friend—
To put forth my best effort—and then,
Hopefully, I can see a harvest come in.
Pray to God that I can help my fellow man,
Because I believe the works that Jesus has done.
So I push forward to see what God can do.

I'm Truly Blessed

I must confess.
I will tell you, my guest:
Put your faith in Jesus before the test.
But you must be saved; this isn't playing chess.
If not, nonetheless, you may still flunk the test.
Honor and favor at their best
Only can come from God—no less.
I'm not special, just blessed.
God gives me faith, favor, authority to pass the test.
Some people call this a spiritual request
Because they don't understand how I can be blessed.
I still deal with sin in my life, I will confess.
This new way of thinking keeps me out of some mess.
But I struggle at times when I'm at my best.
Thank God Jesus won—no less.
Jesus completed God's life test.

The Church

God created the earth.
God helps develop the church.
God works miracles through his church,
God's gifts from heaven to the earth.
God gave birth to the church.
Is church a part of God's heaven on earth?
Why do people go to church?
What is it really worth?
The love of God is why I go to church.
To hear the Word of God is worth the birth of the church.
To see people of all races with the joy of the Lord on their faces
To see love and unity among people is the church.
To see one soul receive salvation from Jesus Christ
Sounds like heaven to me here on earth—
The benefit of knowing God's Word and allowing
it to transform you by God's Word.
If you see God's change in you, then other people
do too; this is the church growing in you.
The church is God's kingdom on earth.
It will prepare you for heaven while you are here on earth.

God's Church Doesn't Restrict Color

Are you my sister or my brother?
God's church doesn't make a difference in people's color.
Do you love God more than you love your mother?
Are you praying, trying to help your sister and brother, yet another?
If God's church doesn't discriminate against color,
why do we treat you this way, my brother?
You are my family from the inward part down to your skin.
Man looks on the outward part, but God looks from within. 1Sam:16-7
Because we get stuck on the skin, we do offend.
If we were blind, would we mind?
Talking to someone's spirit on the phone, we can talk a long time.
But because we can see them, never mind.
God's church never had restriction on the inside.
It seems like children understand.
They see another child and want to play;
Then they may grab them by the hand.
And please, let's destroy our pride;
Let's have fellowship, one with another,
And ask God to help us understand our sister and brother.
Jesus loves our soul; he wants to make us spiritually whole
So the true church of Jesus Christ's love can unfold.

The Tomb

This is a very important part of Jesus's legacy—the tomb,
Walking on water to his disciples who were in the boat.
Jesus is the anchor that kept them afloat,
Healing people all over the earth,
Even healing a blind man who was blind from birth.
Jesus's death and resurrection go hand in hand.
He laid down his life for generations and future
generations; this was God's plan.
Knowing and trusting by faith, God's resurrection brings us hope and grace.
Jesus proclaimed to us over and over again
All the things in the Bible God had commanded.
Just as Jesus commanded Lazarus to rise from the tomb,
Jesus's crucifixion on the cross would happen in Jerusalem very soon.
When Jesus proclaimed, "Destroy this temple, and
in three days, God will raise it up again,"
He was referring to his body, not the building of man.
We may not quite understand.
People saw Jesus beaten for our sins,
Hung on the cross between two thieves—had committed no sin.
Jesus was the Lamb of God who took away the sins of the world,
Died on the cross, put in a tomb.
Was it over, were we to assume?
And in three days was Jesus's prediction too soon.
Either you believe Jesus was risen from the tomb
Or you doubt this fact and you have no room.
Even Jesus's disciples had their doubts and fear
Before Mary visited the tomb and found his body not there.
And he is coming back for his bride, the church, soon.
We come out of the womb.
Then it's our destiny to live life abundantly until we reach the tomb.

A Labor of Love

What is this thing called *labor of love*?
Love shows forth action, I know,
And labor is working out a task.
Let's put the two words *labor* and *love* together and work out a craft.
Whom do you know who has loved and worked for his neighbor?
As I ponder this thought, I can't help but think of my Lord and Savior.
Jesus is symbolic when we talk about *labor of love*.
Jesus honored and obeyed every command God gave
And died for us on Calvary in our place.
God has always shown us examples of the labor of love.
We were made in God's image from his labor of love.
For Adam and Eve, it was all too soon before they fell
out of love with God on their honeymoon.
Has anyone else shared in this labor of love?
I believe some parents take part in the labor of love.
Providing for your family can be a motivating love task.
Jacob in the Bible worked fourteen years because he loved
Rachel and wanted to be married to her. Genesis 29:19-28
And because his love was strong, he felt fourteen years wasn't that long.
Do you live to be loved or live to show love?
I believe the labor of love are these two things:
Love the Lord God with all your heart, mind, soul, and strength,
And love your neighbor as yourself.
The apostle Paul stated that he was a love slave for the gospel of Jesus Christ.
And yes, if you read the New Testament to see how
Paul served Jesus Christ, you will agree.
Paul's love for Jesus outweighed the task.
He continues to overcome difficult circumstances and spread
the gospel throughout the Gentile nations that last.
Daniel was another Bible character who showed the labor of love.
He served God in the heathen nation and worked for the King
Nebuchadnezzar with an excellent attitude and dedication.
In time, Daniel had proven himself more productive than all
administrators and was placed over the entire Babylonian Province.

Some people in church say I am blessed and highly favored.
My question to them is, "Have you turned
around and blessed your neighbor?"
The Good Samaritan was blessed and highly favored because,
to me, he showed mercy to his neighbor. Luke 10:25-37
Have you ever participated in the labor of love?
Because if you have, then you will know its
compassion and act of God's love.

New Testament Now

Thank God for Jesus's New Testament faith.
It has some people going ape.
Jesus followed the law of the land as a man,
Followed God's will without sin.
Jesus is that God covenant made with man.
Jesus will not deny you; that's why he died for you.
I can testify Jesus is the truth.
My life is a testimony, so I can identify
Jesus can save you if you trust Jesus with your heart.
What has God called you to do?
When you give your life to Jesus, you can testify
and grow to what he has for you.
You will be free from sin, no longer a slave from within.
Yes, you will still sin, but the choice is yours, my friend.
Jesus has given us authority over sin; he won that
victory on Calvary way back then
And was also made to save.
Jesus conquered death, hell, and the grave,
Resurrection and new, abundant life.
God has given Jesus authority in heaven and on earth.
But the covenant God has made with man through Jesus is here on earth.

The Lord Is My Shepherd

He knows everything I want.
I am sorry for being so blunt
Because the Lord knows me. Why front?
We are made in God's image.
So what is our dilemma?
The birds sing every day to thank God for making a way.
The trees stand nice and tall, pointing toward heaven before they fall.
The rain falls from heaven to the earth.
Thunder and lightning get our attention as God's
sounds, the sky with a new transition.
So who is your shepherd,
And does he know what you need?
Because anything demonic at this time is not what you should receive.
Do you know what you want, or are you still on the hunt?
Does your shepherd lead you beside strange waters?
Will he lead you on the path of destruction?
Does he give you whatever you want?
When you walk through the shadow of death, does he leave you?
Do you feel fear and doubt shall follow you all the days of your life?
Tell me, which Lord is your shepherd? Psalm:chapter23
This is determined by you,
How you live your life and what you do.
Who is your shepherd, and tell me, what has he done for you?

Why Can't We Receive What God Has Done?

God is the one—
The only one that's greater than the Son.
There are many impostors under the sun.
But there is one God, of whom Jesus is the Son.
That's my God; that's the one who sent Jesus, his only begotten son.
You know Jesus Christ, the anointed one,
The one who people deny
Under the sun.
And Jesus learned to follow God's plan from the beginning to the end.
And you know something else—he never ever did fall into sin.
He spoke and quoted God's Word over and over again.
He lived the life God wanted him to live; that's why he never sinned.
Jesus's love for God was much greater than sin.
Jesus prayed to God every day to make sure he was
following God's commands each day.
He prayed to God one day, and God gave him
twelve disciples to show the way.
Jesus did what God wanted him to do.
Because of this, God granted miracles of the truth.
People know that God was with him
Because everything Jesus did, God showed proof.
Everything God wanted to happen in the earth,
Jesus was God's number-one man from birth.
Heaven's reflection of Jesus on earth shows that
he had spiritual authority in his words.
He was not like any man.
He had God's love, power, and authority throughout the land.
People who believed in what God would do
Received miracles from Jesus; that's God's living truth.
You can receive from God this day
If you open your mouth and pray.

Ask God to forgive your sins; then ask Jesus to come
into your heart, to save you from sin.
And this will be the best thing you have ever done with your life.
Trust God and continue to pray,
And Jesus will always show you the way.

God Is Not on Our Level

Did you know God has defeated the devil?
And God has defeated him on all levels.
No, God isn't insane; he remains in dominion over man.
Some people think the devil is on God's level.
God never has and never will be on Satan's level.
There are many Gods in the land,
But only one who created the heavens and earth and man.
God owns every living thing.
Is that why all creation sings—to worship and
praise, to acknowledge our king?
What doesn't God own? I would really like to know.
If you think God is on your level,
Who then has authority over the devil?
God formed Jesus into human flesh.
Jesus honored God, served each command.
Jesus took back heaven's authority on earth from the devil as a man
Because Adam and Eve lost the title to the kingdom of God as a rebel.
And God even owns the devil
Because he was under God's authority as an angel in the beginning.
So God has authority over good and evil,
And the devil has to get permission from God
before he goes on a mission. Job1:6-12
Did you not know God created human birth?
So what are some of our misconceptions on the earth?
We can't even compare, so please, let's take our nose out of the air.
And don't forget our ego, amigo.
When will people wake up and see God for who he really is?
God, we pray your will be done on earth as it
is in heaven, Matthew chapter 6:
Jesus came to earth to connect us back to God through his birth.

God's Helping Hand

Thank God for his helping hand
Because you better believe it, if you are a man.
Jesus Christ came as a baby, not a man.
Some people don't believe God's merciful hand.
Some folks say, "Why would he extend it to man?"
To share himself with man.
To help us grow is a part of God's love for man.
But the devil didn't deceive Adam and Eve.
Eve was deceived, Adam shared the fruit, and they both got the boot.
Now, where does this leave you and me?
The devil is good at deceiving mankind.
That's why some people are spiritually imprisoned in their mind.
But God sent Jesus into this cruel world
To help redeem men, women, boys, and girls.
Jesus is God's only begotten son.
Some people don't believe he has come.
Others believe in a false one.
No one has died for our guilt, sin, and shame.
Jesus died on the cross for our sins so we can be saved.
There is power in the love of God
Because Calvary for Jesus Christ is and will always be for us.
Jesus paid a price so we can believe and receive life,
The abundant life, through Jesus Christ.
Abundant life is this paradise.
On earth, you better believe that's right.
May your will be done on earth
As the Holy Spirit directs us in our new birth.
God can give us help; that's what people in the Bible pray to God about.
God always will send you what you need.
God's love is real.

God Wants to Take You Higher

Are you inspired?
Does this start a fire?
Do you want to go higher?
Is this your one desire?
No, I'm not a liar.
God can really take you higher
To reach your soul desirer.
Do you want to live where God has required?
And I don't mean to build your own empire.
I mean to follow God as the Holy Spirit encourages your heart's desire.
On what level do you admire?
It's not about you; it's God's love for you to take you higher.
God can help you become all that he requires.
There is only one thing that can expire: the time
you don't spend with Jesus to go higher.

The Legend

Who are the legends?
Does your suspense have you thinking,
And who might this person be?
We may be thinking and looking in the same direction.
What qualifies you to be a legend?
And do you know anybody who can complete this application?
And do they live in our community or in our nation?
Are they still living, or have they died and had a cremation?
Please be patient; I will digress with this information.
I will give you an illustration.
But before I disclose this information,
Close your eyes, and have a moment of meditation.
If you were birthed on earth
And are helping others thrive,
Then you are a legend, the untold story.
Maybe you disagree with me.
But let me finish so you can see all of the possibilities.
God chose you from birth to give you an opportunity on earth,
To reach you and teach you to connect with you.
You were made in his image; that's legendary
right there, from the beginning.
So how's your progress now that you are living?
Are you willing to know and grow into God's destiny?
This means you must deny yourself
And surrender to God.
Once you are walking in God's spiritual path,
You are God's legend now; you are living life with God's purpose.
Each day is a testimony of whose you are.
This comes from God, that spiritual heritage, so now that you know
you are a legend, and if you are faithfully prepared for life's mission,
Ordained and not ashamed,
Then you are that next living legend; walk humbly in Jesus's name.

Printed in the United States
by Baker & Taylor Publisher Services